Natural Timber Frame Homes

Natural Timber Frame Homes

BUILDING WITH WOOD, STONE, CLAY, AND STRAW

WAYNE J. BINGHAM

JEROD PFEFFER

Gibbs Smith, Publisher
TO ENRICH AND INSPIRE HUMANKIND

Salt Lake City | Charleston | Santa Fe | Santa Barbara

First Edition

11 10 09 08 07   5 4 3 2 1

Published by

Gibbs Smith, Publisher

PO Box 667

Layton, Utah 84041

Orders: 1.800.835.4993

www.gibbs-smith.com

Designed by Johnson Design, Inc.

Produced by TTA Design

Printed and bound in China

Library of Congress Cataloging-in-Publication Data

Bingham, Wayne J.
Natural timber frame homes: building with wood, stone, clay, and straw / Wayne J. Bingham, Jerod Pfeffer. — 1st ed.
  p. cm.
ISBN-13: 978-1-58685-860-5
ISBN-10: 1-58685-860-2
 1. Wooden-frame houses. 2. Building materials. 3. Appropriate technology. I. Pfeffer, Jerod. II. Title.

TH4818.W6.B485 2007
690'.837—dc22

2006026250

For Colleen, Michelle, David, Christopher, Jon, Mary, and Michael.

—Wayne J. Bingham

For Sage, whose smile has given me true shelter.

—Jerod Pfeffer

Contents

Acknowledgments

Building with natural, locally available materials feels like an ideological leap in an age of chipboard and vinyl. Yet this book is really a continuation of the job started with the first human shelter and developed by millennia of trial and error into the modern timber frame and straw wall. We owe a great debt to our ancestors for the accumulated knowledge of turning trees, stones, and mud into durable and beautiful shelters.

While traveling to capture images for this book, we were met with great enthusiasm and given gracious access to personal living spaces at every doorstep we visited, sometimes on very short notice. Thank you to the owners and builders who made their natural homes, their experiences, and their time available to us during this project. We are inspired by the level of craftsmanship being brought to contemporary natural buildings. We are especially grateful to Stormy and JJ Colman, Gilbert Geauthreau, Lynn and Derrick Goldberg, Chuck and Anne Hanson, Fran Hart, Alan and Linda Klagge, the Lama Foundation, Eric and Teresa Malone, Mark and Katie Waller, and Greg Weeks.

Kari Bremer of Natural & Green Design and Mark Giorgetti of Palo Santo Designs gave new meaning to the phrase *above and beyond* by giving generously of their time, ideas, and good company. Many of the homes presented in this book are the products of their fine craftsmanship.

Eric Malone and Eric Husted of Lorax Forest Care supplied us with access to their strawbale and timber frame homes and shared a vision of forestry as a solution instead of a problem. Thank you to Eric and Eric for showing us that sustainable wood products are both possible and practical.

For logistical assistance, insight, and inspiration, we are indebted to Kelly Ray Mathews, Werner Heiber, Gene Leone, and John Murray.

We are greatly indebted to the writings of Wendell Berry for perspective, inspiration, and hope.

Putting together a book is in many ways like building a house, proceeding from foundation to finish work. Without the original support of Gibbs Smith, Publisher, CEO Christopher Robbins, this book would never have become a reality. A big thank-you to our editor Aimee Stoddard for planing off the rough spots in the manuscript and asking questions where they needed to be asked.

Thank you to Colleen Smith for proofreading several versions of the book, for becoming part of the production team at the eleventh hour, for handling many of the logistical issues involved in traveling around the country, for delivering well-timed and tasty calories to weary authors, and for putting up with two people talking about nothing but natural building.

Thank you to Sage Hibberd for offering feedback through a long winter of writing, for continuing to be a natural builder while her partner was off being a writer, for handling all the parts of life that still need tending to when a person is focused on only one thing, and for her enthusiasm for the book and encouragement.

Finally, we are grateful we had the opportunity to build our own wood, stone, clay, and straw homes. The ideas presented in this book are the direct result of our own trials, frequent errors, and sometimes surprising successes.

Porch roof supported with post and knee braces.

The strong grain of oak timber frame bents stands out from the earthen plaster.

Introduction

Have you peace, the quiet urge that reveals your power?
Have you remembrances, the glimmering arches that span the
summits of the mind?
Have you beauty, that leads the heart from things fashioned of
wood and stone to the holy mountain?
Tell me, have you these in your houses?
—Kahlil Gibran, *The Prophet*

The twenty-first century is a unique time to be human and in need of shelter. We can build anything that our imagination, determination, and pocketbooks will allow. The global economy has given us access to resources from everywhere: tropical hardwoods, imported metals, and exotic stone. Industry has made possible every conceivable product, including synthetic floors, roofs, and windows. Fossil fuels have allowed us to heat and cool increasingly larger houses.

We have created a building system that implies no limits other than price.

An examination of the larger range of evidence, however, suggests that we have not properly accounted for the effect of our building systems on climatic stability, air quality, water quality, ecosystems, and biodiversity. Scientists are warning us that instead of happening sometime in future decades, climate change resulting from carbon-dioxide emissions has already begun. In the sunshine of cheap energy, we have allowed ourselves to believe that we are not constrained by the laws that govern the natural world.

Paralleling the climate change associated with burning petroleum is its rising price.

Heating and cooling our inefficient structures is getting costly, and the problem will intensify as the petroleum supply diminishes. It is now increasingly difficult for some people to supply their home with adequate heat and air-conditioning. Political instability has strained the capacity of industrial nations to secure oil acquisition and a transit system, and this strain is felt in the price we pay for all commodities.

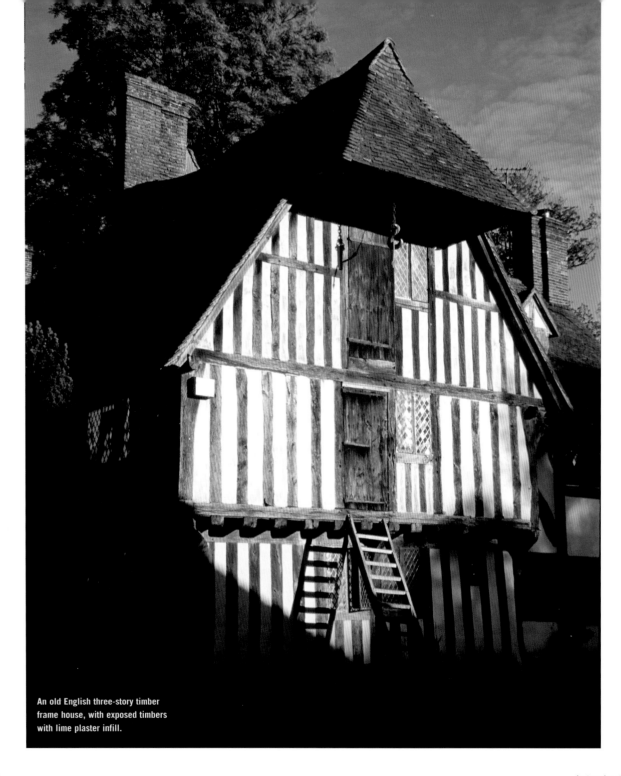

An old English three-story timber frame house, with exposed timbers with lime plaster infill.

An adobe interior wall provides thermal mass to a timber frame kitchen.

Synthetic stucco and manmade stone make up the townhome exteriors in a new, conventional building project.

America's Approach to Building

Building your own home with local materials is not a new idea. In fact, it has been the only approach of humans and other animals for most of history. However, as we have shifted the responsibility for building houses from ourselves and our community to industry, our involvement in building has declined, and the monetary cost has greatly increased. We pay hundreds of thousands of dollars, and because most homes are not built to last, houses are not the long-term investments they once were.

The poor quality of our houses is not primarily the fault of careless contractors, but instead the result of a building system designed to produce such a house. Low-quality, expensive dwellings are a product of the system functioning well. By giving over the responsibility of providing our own shelter to an industry, the house has moved from a personal creation to a commodity—not designed to be durable, beautiful, and efficient, but to encourage consumption. It is telling that the health of the housing industry

on a national level is measured by the total number of homes built each year—an indication of one thing: quantity.

As our standard of living continues to rise—evidenced by bigger homes equipped with more conveniences—there has been a steady decline since World War II in the number of us who admit to leading satisfied lives. If more and bigger things really made us happy, the percentage should be getting higher. Why has the growing number of material goods left us unfulfilled?

Roses and ivy greet pedestrians in an English community.

The answer is very much wrapped up in the way we conduct our lives. It is not irrational that we feel disconnected, marginalized, and isolated, and that "we don't know who we are"; this feeling is in many ways accurate. If who we are is defined by the relationships between us and other people, us and our food, us and our homes, then there are some large holes in our self-awareness.

Sources of Materials

It is clear from the growing popularity of food co-ops, farmers markets, small breweries, and pottery studios that a segment of the population is seeking out the stories of their purchases. When we buy from department stores and lumberyards, we know only a small part of any item's history. The foremost question is, "How much does it cost?" Price is the primary consideration in an industrial economy because the anonymity of distant production and distribution allows us to think of all two-by-fours as the same.

Every product has a story. But because the siding, plywood, light fixtures, concrete, and other home products we buy are manufactured so far from our doorstep, the job of telling their story is left to advertisers. They promise fulfillment, happiness, pleasure, and social grace, but deliver little in the way of genuine meaning.

Above: Timbers and planks air drying without energy-intensive kilns.
Below: Trees in a healthy forest can be thinned selectively, maintaining the health and longevity of the woodlot.

Conventional buildings rely on lumber transported great distances at high environmental and economic cost.

Textured plaster and smooth timber add visual interest and welcome visitors.

Local Materials and Renewable Energy

Our solution is both simple and radical: build with locally available materials and renewable energy. By using local wood and straw, we can become involved in the entire building process and be certain that it aligns with our values. In the global marketplace, such an accounting is nearly impossible.

Explore the place where you live. Are there forests nearby? What trees grow there? How much can you draw from the natural world without depleting it? Who can help you build? To be able to answer these questions is to be able to envision a sustainable future.

We argue in this book for drawing the support for your life from the place where you live. If our fuel, lumber, or food comes from somewhere else, we can only live comfortably to the extent that we are economically or politically powerful.

Leaving the world as good as or better than we found it is a personal and public responsibility. Industrial materials are profitable in a narrow sense, but the pollution, the high monetary cost, and the homogenizing effect on building are bankrupting our social landscape and cultural commons.

The belief that ordinary people cannot build houses without contractors has recently gained wide acceptance. Human history, however, richly illustrates the opposite: constructing our own shelter is not only possible, it reconnects us to the natural world in ways that we crave.

There are people everywhere, often without previous construction experience, discovering their ability to build. They are using local, recycled, and salvaged materials to construct inexpensive and beautiful homes. In the process, they are developing fit bodies, discovering unknown skills, and cultivating a feeling of independence.

The frame of a two-hundred-year-old barn demonstrates the integrity of traditional building methods.

Challenging Basic Assumptions

A building truly begins not with backhoes and shovels but with our assumptions. Our core beliefs have great influence on our perception of the costs and benefits associated with building, our selection of appropriate materials, our prioritization of values, and ultimately the character of the finished house. To design a sustainable building, think of the starting point of a house not as meeting with the architect or digging a hole, but as identifying and challenging your assumptions.

In this chapter, we lay the foundation of our proposal to build with locally available, unprocessed materials. We do this for two reasons: first, to demonstrate that all building systems are the end products of our assumptions about how we fit into the world; and second, to demonstrate that the dramatic changes to the conventional system we propose are both necessary and practical.

The ideas presented are based on five assumptions:

1. Life is possible without oil.
2. Human health results from environmental health.
3. Building is an economic opportunity.
4. Direct involvement has financial and personal rewards.
5. Natural materials plus human hands equals beautiful houses.

An old timber frame barn exudes strength and durability and offers important lessons for contemporary builders.

Round log rafters are supported by a timber frame in a kitchen that is seen through an arched opening in an adobe thermal wall.

Challenging Basic Assumptions

A soapstone masonry heater separates the dining area from the kitchen and hallway. Round log beams incorporated into the timber frame articulate the space.

Challenging Basic Assumptions

A centuries-old timber frame infilled with earthen and lime plaster supports the thatch roof of this English home.

Life Without Oil

Humans built homes, grew food, and moved across continents long before the discovery of fossil fuels. Today, however, the construction industry is dependent on imported energy to manufacture and transport concrete, metal, gypsum board, plywood, vinyl siding, glass, and virtually all other building products. The heavy equipment and power tools used to construct a conventional house require gas and electricity. Over their lifetime, finished houses additionally require large amounts of energy for lighting, heating, cooling, and operating appliances.

We can build differently. Because of the apparent low cost of energy, there has been little incentive to consider alternatives to oil when designing houses. The true costs of building, owning, and operating houses have not been readily apparent, and so it has seemed less expensive to approach these issues in commonly accepted ways. Instead of critically analyzing the natural charac-teristics of the site and incorporating passive heating and cooling strategies, the contemporary builder has been able to use mechanical systems to compensate for design inadequacies.

Today, we see houses in cold climates with garages on the south side, blocking all solar gain. We see desert homes with thin stick-framed walls that require air-conditioning to cool. Houses have become very much disconnected from their place

Challenging Basic Assumptions

in the natural world. Oil has allowed us to mask the inappropriateness of structures by putting in more energy, allowing all styles of housing to be built almost anywhere, essentially treating all places as the same place.

Building a post-oil house is much the same as building a pre-oil house. We have some excellent examples from around the world. Japan and Europe possess a rich heritage of timber frame and natural insulation use. Their traditions inform us about how to build, but because these structures are a response to climate and culture, we need to adapt historical systems to our locally available materials.

Natural building is the process of finding what is unique—a pursuit of the most appropriate response to climate, culture, and materials. Snowy areas will experience climate in similar ways and can certainly share strategies. Yet the trees, rocks, type of clay, amount of sun, and occupations and needs of the people will all be different. Within a specific community, each individual will experience differences in solar exposure, material availability, need for space, and sense of aesthetics. The best natural buildings are those that most fully incorporate their occupants' needs, culture, climate, and available solar energy.

A timber frame entrance with a thatch roof leads into the cottage.

Detail of timber frame with mortise-and-tenon joints that do not require bolts and can be designed to resist lateral forces.

Challenging Basic Assumptions

Environmental and Human Health

We have a practical and ethical obligation to preserve ecosystems: practical because our food, air, and water are the products of ecosystem functions; ethical because we are not the first humans to inhabit this planet and should not rightly make ourselves the last.

Walking the aisles of home-improvement superstores, it is easy to forget that building products result primarily from biological processes. Plywood does not begin its life in factories; it begins as a tree in the forest. When the productive capacity of the forest is reduced through clear-cutting or soil erosion, we jeopardize material availability in the future. A responsible builder is by necessity a naturalist.

We cannot be healthy if we live in a sick environment because we are in a constant exchange of nutrients with our environment. Poisons in the air and water eventually enter and poison our bodies. It follows that our primary environment—the house—must be constructed of nontoxic materials.

A lone tree standing in a harvested wheat field on a small, diverse farm.

Diverse and Stable Economies

Your dollar is a vote. By withholding or redirecting your participation, you have the power to influence economic systems and support sustainable enterprise. By building naturally and locally, you support grain farmers, small sawmills, and loggers. You promote a broad set of values, such as stable economies, diverse landscapes, local jobs, and community. Building a house is—for most of us—the biggest economic interaction of our life. Material choices have enormous potential to move us from an industrial to a biological economy.

The "success" of the industrial system has been to remove the history and therefore the ethics from purchasing. This scenario has been a great obstacle to a sustainable society because the manufacture and transportation of all products have very real effects on people and the environment. By accepting responsibility for these effects and by searching out economic interactions that support farms and forests instead of smokestacks, we can acquire the tools to build a stable economy and healthy community.

Natural building is an opportunity to learn valuable skills and build community.

Challenging Basic Assumptions

Locally harvested logs cut by a portable sawmill provide the wood for a natural timber frame.

Benefits of Building Your Own Home

In his thorough and imaginative book *Mortgage Free!,* Rob Roy puts our current wages-for-house structure into perspective:

> In the Middle Ages, tenant farmers worked three months of the year for the lord of the estate. In return, they got land, house, and the advantages of the communal defense system. Three months. And we call these people serfs. In grade school, we thought of serfdom as only slightly removed from slavery. Yet in my home state of New York, 'Tax Freedom Day' is in late May. We work the first 140-odd days of the year just to pay local, state, and federal taxes . . . and we still haven't done anything about the shelter itself. With roughly a third of the average after-tax middle-class income going toward housing, we can conservatively add another 90 days to reach 'Shelter Freedom Day' sometime in late August. So now we're committed to eight months labor to achieve what the peasants of the Middle Ages accomplished by their three-month contract with their lords. If those poor wretches were serfs, what word can we find to describe ourselves?

A lime-plastered, thatched-roofed cottage shows the beauty of natural materials and building by hand.

Challenging Basic Assumptions

Earthen plaster over strawbale walls complements an oak timber frame.

A niche cut in the strawbale wall adds a sculptural element to the earthen plaster.

A wood-framed truth window shows strawbale laid on edge with twine exposed on the surface.

Of course, serfs didn't have two-car garages and Jacuzzi bathtubs, but it is worth asking a fundamental question: Is the way we build and pay for houses worth that much of our working lives?

Reducing cost is a compelling reason to become involved in the construction of your house. By eliminating the labor and profit of contractors and by utilizing local materials, a home can be built for a fraction of the conventional cost. Another reason to construct your own home is the satisfaction that is to be gained from being physically involved in something of primary value to your life. A measure of independence and freedom is gained by knowing how to shelter yourself.

Building is deeply satisfying work. You are never in doubt of what you accomplished in a day because the evidence is right there before you. If you do your work well, you leave a meaningful legacy to those who will follow.

Challenging Basic Assumptions

Wood beautifully complements
hand-applied earthen plaster.

Challenging Basic Assumptions

Wood, adobe, and earthen-plastered strawbale walls give richness and character to a natural timber frame home.

Challenging Basic Assumptions

The frame and roof can be assembled first to protect straw walls from weather.

Challenging Basic Assumptions

Challenging Basic Assumptions

Beautiful, Natural, Hand-Built Homes

Most of us have experienced extraordinary buildings. Perhaps it was a national park lodge with soaring log trusses and weathered siding, a stone church, a centuries-old European village, a rustic cabin on a lake, or a working barn. These places hold magnetic charm largely absent from uniform and predictable contemporary structures. Made largely by human hands and natural materials, these buildings somehow resonate with us.

Beauty is a subjective concept, but clearly the materials we choose and the spirit in which we work contribute to the feeling of the finished building. We, of course, have no scientific studies proving that natural materials possess more beauty—a quality much less objective than rate of heat flow or square feet. Yet we feel confident that natural building materials are physically and emotionally healthier than highly processed and synthetically based alternatives.

A table saw can easily repeat precise cuts in a way challenging to even the best of craftsmen with a handsaw. Factories can chip and glue wood to produce arrow-straight framing material. Is it reasonable to wonder if the products of the human craftsperson are inherently inferior to industrial materials?

The graceful arches of this abandoned church in Wales demonstrate the skill of medieval craftsmen, who used hand tools, and the longevity of stone structures.

Challenging Basic Assumptions

A handcrafted English stone house, with thatch roof, demonstrates richness of natural materials.

Machines and human hands are suited to different tasks. Interchangeable parts spawned the industrial revolution, and it is within this context that flat planes and exact replication are valued.

The comparison of humans and machines is not based on the assumption that machines are better humans, but that humans are inferior machines. But no machine exists that can enjoy the taste of homemade bread or take satisfaction in accomplishment. Natural building is a decidedly human undertaking, its refinement not a result of increasing uniformity, but of practice and understanding.

Diversity does not make us inferior to machines; it is the expression of our humanity. If we judge a building's suitability as a human dwelling instead of its compatibility with the industry of building, we can view our relationship to machines in a different light.

Developers can decrease material and labor costs by perceiving all places as the same place, all houses as the same house, all people as average people. Yet if your house is a replica, how do you differentiate your life from the lives of your neighbors? Does the industrial system really serve our needs or have our needs been made subordinate to the needs of the system?

A round-wood, mortise-and-tenon bed frame uses construction techniques similar to a timber frame home.

Challenging Basic Assumptions

A stairwell, flooded with natural light, is articulated by the timber frame and thick earthen-plastered strawbale walls.

Details, such as curved tenons, give each timber frame a unique character.

Challenging Basic Assumptions

A cottage roof shows the sculptural quality of thatch.

Evaluating the Problem
of Conventional Building

The totality with which we have committed ourselves to fossil fuels is astonishing. From food production to transportation, to building and heating our homes, virtually no part of modern industrial life is unsupported by oil. Centralized factories use large amounts of energy to convert natural materials into uniform sheets of plywood, metal roofing, glass, asphalt shingles, cement, tile, paint, tar paper, nails, bolts, electrical and plumbing fixtures, heating devices, bricks, molding, and so on. And without diesel trucks and cargo ships, these products would never make it to our door.

Is oil a reliable foundation for our society?

Geologists and common sense, however, tell us that oil will not last forever. Climate scientists are warning us that the benefits already obtained from fossil energy have come at too high of a price. For the first time in history, humans have altered climate to the extent that the future of our species is uncertain. A majority of the forest, animal, plant, wetland, and ocean ecosystems that we depend on for fresh water, oxygen, and food are in decline. Overcutting of timber, pollution buildup, topsoil loss, and climate change are degrading the natural systems that make our existence possible.

The official solution has been to intensify production, expand oil exploration, and increase subsidy, which has met with the same success that eating more quickly has on food shortages. In the face of lessening oil

supply and rising cost, we are adding more cars to the road, building bigger houses, and shipping our food greater distances. Demand for oil is growing at the same time as the emerging economic powers China and India seek to adopt a standard of living comparable to Western countries.

Costly energy will cripple our economy not because a large amount is a prerequisite for human survival, but because, over the last several decades, we have been promoting a global economy that makes abundant, cheap energy a necessity. We have designed an economic system that can only exist in a kind of energy fairy tale, where oil wells never run dry and pollution has no ill effect on climate or people.

The reality is quite different. We will at some point run out of oil. In some ways, we

Cement plants emit one ton of carbon dioxide for each ton of finished cement.

have already. Even if the last drop has not been pumped from the ground, the carbon dioxide released by burning fossil fuels is jeopardizing the climate system of the earth and therefore has limited viability as a present and future source of fuel. It is also worth asking if exhausting the global supply of anything is in our best interests or ethically acceptable. Generations to come may discover new applications for oil, but find that all reserves have been depleted. We have already used more than our fair share.

We conventionally define building in such narrow economic and aesthetic terms that we have undervalued our surroundings, the health of our own bodies, the true costs of production, the future, and building itself.

Evaluating the Problem of Conventional Building

We are now facing some serious ecological realities:

- The climate that makes life on earth possible is changing due to human activity. The scientific consensus is that global warming will lead to an increase in disease and violent storms and less biological stability.
- We have seriously poisoned our air and water. The body of every person on the planet contains chemicals not known one hundred years ago.
- A majority of the forest, animal, plant, wetland, and ocean ecosystems that we depend on for fresh water, oxygen, and food are in decline. Overcutting of timber, pollution buildup, topsoil loss, and climate change are degrading the natural systems that make our existence possible.
- Our culture is dependent on nonrenewable fuels for food, shelter, and almost everything else, and these fuels are becoming more costly.
- The burning of these fuels is making the planet less habitable for humans and other life. Our system of living gives personal and environmental degradation the appearance of necessity.
- The construction and fueling of buildings is a primary contributor to the problem.

A forest after clear cutting—the method used to obtain most conventional framing lumber.

Evaluating the Problem of Conventional Building

Extraction of metal bearing ore created this manmade crater.

Evaluating the Problem of Conventional Building

Power to run tools and heat and light homes is transported great distances from its source.

Transporting materials from the factory to the building site requires enormous amounts of energy.

Refining plants convert oil into fuel for trucks and railroads, which transport conventional building materials from the factory to the lumberyard.

Evaluating the Problem of Conventional Building

Delivery of industrial materials depends on large vehicles that consume fossil fuels.

When the short lifecycle of industrial materials is over, large machines are required to manage ever-increasing landfills.

Evaluating the Problem of Conventional Building

Toxic Interior Environments

There is increasing evidence that the highly processed materials used in conventional construction negatively affect our health—due both to their toxic ingredients and their inability to pass water vapor. The combination of highly sealed houses, "un-breathable" materials such as plywood and foam, and water vapor from baths and kitchens results in condensation in walls. Mold growth from trapped water is a growing health problem in new homes. The paints, carpets, caulks, plywood, pipes, and furniture that fill modern homes emit volatile organic compounds in the form of toxic fumes that cause illness.

Impact of Conventional Building

Conventional building is more expensive than you might imagine. The cost of pollution in the production of materials, the cost of climate change, the cost of heavy equipment on soils, the cost of mining activities for roofing, siding, and wires on landscapes are charged to future generations.

We cannot, however, pass on the direct monetary cost of a conventional house. A $200,000 mortgage at 6 percent interest will cost you $430,000 over thirty years. Your life and energy must be directed to paying that amount back to the lender—placing some serious limits on the way you can live.

Conventional building materials come from "somewhere else." Most of us do not know how they were extracted from the environment, manufactured, or delivered.

Evaluating the Problem of Conventional Building

The bank will give you some negative feedback if you decide to spend more time with your kids, growing your food, or becoming active in local government and less time working to pay off your home mortgage.

The industrial economy gives incentives that work against sustainability in three primary ways:

1. Every place in the world becomes our shopping center. We lose the concept that places other than our own have cultural and ecological value apart from their natural resources.
2. We feel only arbitrary ecological and social limits. If the entire world is at our fingertips there is little incentive to live within ecological limits. We can always get what we need somewhere else. Abundant somewhere else's are, however, becoming less available for plunder.
3. We cannot personally experience or measure impacts. We have to rely on industry itself, the media, and "watchdog" groups to mitigate problems and place our actions within a biological context.

The use of highly processed materials and complex construction techniques separate sealed glass and steel buildings from the natural world.

When we buy a 2 x 4 from the lumberyard, we do not see the effect on the forest.

Evaluating the Problem of Conventional Building

Industrial materials do not biodegrade after their useful life is over. Replacing a twenty-five-year-old highway overpass produces a tremendous volume of twisted rebar and concrete waste.

Evaluating the Problem of Conventional Building

Owner Involvement in a Building Project

Despite the fact that many of the world's inhabitants still build their own homes, it is not very common in the United States. One reason for this is that building has become quite complicated from a material standpoint. The electrical, plumbing, framing, foundation, and roof systems require specialized tools and skills. Some tasks, such as wiring a house, involve a degree of danger that would put an unskilled person in an unacceptably risky situation.

Another reason is that we have embraced the idea of specialization. In the industrial economy, we have divided ourselves into specialties (doctors, truck drivers, politicians, and so on) and for the most part, we do one thing and leave our food production, entertainment, and home construction to other specialists. This scenario has been—to a great degree—the result of fossil fuel use. Centralization and specialization are a logical outcome of inexpensive transportation. When food and other materials could be shipped long distances, fewer and fewer individuals or companies were needed to produce them.

This is the economic system that produces the conventional house. It has given us many things—reliable drinking water, sewer systems, and conveniences such as clothes washers and electric ovens. These advances, however, have come at a price. Our houses now take the better part of our working lives to pay for, are toxic to the point of affecting our health, and are entirely dependent on fossil fuel use for their basic functions.

Heavy equipment is expensive to hire and disruptive to soil.

Evaluating the Problem of Conventional Building

The conventional home is complicated and relies on materials from unknown sources.

An artistically braced porch invites visitors into this thatched-roof cottage.

Differences Between Conventional and Naturally Built Houses

There is a reason that a restored 1800s brick farmhouse evokes more beauty than a vinyl-sided split-level in the suburbs. Because building products have been converted from natural materials to products of industry, they possess a uniformity that is anathema to the subtleties of real people. Natural materials have intrinsic character. They are essentially the natural world that has been collected and rearranged to provide a human dwelling.

The central case of this book is this: if you desire a beautiful, healthy, affordable house, one that can construct you with simple tools, a house that respects ecological limits, build with local materials.

Only by using materials found in your area can you know the ecological limits. Only by supporting local products can you have a clear understanding of the source, creation, and disposal. By engaging the

This double car garage with the home behind welcomes the automobile more than the occupants.

places that we live in this way, we start to develop an ecological language. We add words to our vocabulary that enable us to discuss and interpret the natural world in more complex and valuable ways. Sourcing materials locally gives us a context in which we can make decisions. We can see both the costs and the benefits more clearly. Finally, by taking our living from our immediate surroundings, we come to know, value, and hopefully protect the places that we live.

Evaluating the Problem of Conventional Building

Repetition of the same shape and size are characteristic of industrial development.

Ivy covers the lime plaster and clay tile roof.

Evaluating the Problem of Conventional Building

Above: This single-family dwelling takes a large share of the earth's resources to provide shelter.
Below: Local stone and lime plaster beautifully support a locally harvested thatch roof.

Evaluating the Problem of Conventional Building

Making the Case for Natural Timber Frames

Natural timber frames are built with unprocessed materials such as wood, stone, clay, and straw. The design and construction of a building can be natural as well. By reprioritization of our assumptions, we can weight our building system toward sustainability.

The industrial economy makes judging the impacts of building materials very difficult by spreading extraction, production, and transportation over great distances. We cannot see the whole life of a product and consequently have difficulty matching values to purchasing decisions. Because an environmental ethic is beginning to form in the building community and many homeowners are concerned about the impact of toxic materials on their health, "green" versions of insulation, paint, concrete, plywood, roofing, caulks, sealers, and other products are becoming available. Many are undoubtedly better for your health and the environment than the conventional alternatives. Yet where they fail to supply us with a clear picture of sustainability is in their distant manufacture. The same energy is required to move both conventional and "green" products across the country or world, and because we cannot see the source of the materials, we do not perceive ecological limits. We suggest that finding and utilizing local materials provides solutions to a much broader range of economic and environmental problems.

A round-wood, post-and-beam pavilion in a healthy, old-growth forest.

In this chapter, we explore the potential of natural building in the areas of environment, personal health, economics, connections, and aesthetics. We examine how challenging our underlying beliefs about our needs and available resources can provide a useful context for redesigning our approach to building. The questions of which materials to use and how to put them together are inextricably tied to place.

Making the Case for Natural Timber Frames

Various growth stages of wheat and barley, which yield straw as a by-product of grain harvest.

Making the Case for Natural Timber Frames

44

Selective cutting allows for both natural timber frames and healthy forests.

Protection of Our Place

At the end of their life as a house, straw, clay, and timber are better than manufactured products because they are unprocessed and naturally return to the soil. They do not become a waste product because they are food for other ecological systems. Wood and straw are nutrient sources for soil organisms and other plants; clay can be used in another building or returned to its source.

A natural house will quickly return to the soil and become food for a new generation of trees and other plants if not protected from rain. This system of recycling is far more elegant than melting down plastic because it uses only solar power and produces no pollutants. Centuries of continuous occupancy has proven well-crafted natural structures to be extremely durable.

Locally sourced and minimally processed materials use less energy than their industrial counterparts. Consider the example of logging. A tree cut with a chain saw and pulled from the forest with heavy equipment requires a certain amount of gasoline for the saw and diesel for the skidder. The same tree cut with an ax and pulled by a horse also requires energy—although with two important distinctions: the second scenario uses far less energy and the amount that is used comes from renewable, nonpolluting sources. The ax uses human energy, which burns calories from lunch. The horse uses solar energy as well, supplied by the hay the horse has eaten.

A home of dry-stacked stone returns gracefully to the earth after its useful life is over.

This is an important distinction. Energy must be evaluated by the quantity used and, just as importantly, by its source. Using a larger amount of renewable energy, such as human, solar, or wind, is better than using a smaller amount of coal, natural gas, oil, or diesel.

Materials from your bioregion will—by virtue of proximity—use less fuel for transport. If you live in a wooded area, it is ideal to use trees from nearby or from the site to build your timber frame. They can be cut, dried, and transformed into timber on-site with simple tools and human hands.

Most commercial framing lumber has been partially kiln dried to bring the moisture content within a range that will minimize warping and twisting. Traditional timber framers design joinery to minimize movement of green wood rather than relying on energy-intensive kilns. They work during cool parts of the year or store timber in the shade to slow evaporation and use housings to prevent twisting.

Natural building predates cordless drills and chop saws. Because traditional systems evolved with hand tools, they minimize the necessity and importance of machines. Timber framers use all wooden joinery that can be cut with a saw and chisel. Straw insulation and clay plaster are worked with hands and feet.

Boards from selectively cut logs air dry after milling.

Industrial efficiency is typically measured at point of use. For example, a gas water heater is considered efficient because a high percentage of its energy is converted into heat and transferred to water. Very little pollution is produced by the appliance, but the gas extraction, impacts of pipeline transport, and addition of fossil carbon to the atmosphere are left out of the equation.

The natural timber frame is an efficient building system in a biological sense. By using local natural materials, no waste is produced. After constructing the frame, leftover wood cutoffs are used for heating or cooking. Wood is not 100 percent efficient at the point of use; ash remains after burning. But it is 100 percent efficient in a biological sense because ash contains many minerals that can be added to the garden for fertility, used to make soap, or used as an additive for plaster. Building products such as foam and vinyl siding create waste because they have no other use than as insulation and siding.

Building a natural house does not require trashcans and dumpsters. Wood can be grown next to your house. It requires no trucks, pipelines, or wells to distribute and cannot be spilled. Propane production cannot be incorporated into your landscaping plan like a wood lot. Straw remaining after walls and plaster are complete also has a place in the landscape. It can serve as great mulch for

A natural timber frame cut from local fir and pine, with artistically positioned round wood beam and knee brace.

Making the Case for Natural Timber Frames

A handmade ladder leads to sleeping loft in small timber frame with clay/straw wall.

Making the Case for Natural Timber Frames

trees or as a soil cover for areas disturbed in the building process. Excess clay can be used to line a small pond, returned to its source, or saved for another project.

Americans are beginning to hesitantly acknowledge that we live within ecological limits. A building system that recognizes the sources of our materials gives us the feedback necessary to live within those limits. By using the materials on your land or from nearby, it is possible to see more directly the effects of building on forests and fields and protect them.

Local timber uses less energy because it is obtained locally, requiring less transportation, because it is not kiln dried with petroleum, and because it is taken from tree to timber with human, not industrial, power.

A Japanese inn demonstrates the inherent beauty of centuries-old timber framing techniques.

Timber cutoffs can be utilized as a heat source for the home.

A portable saw can mill timbers in close proximity to the building site.

Making the Case for Natural Timber Frames

Ceramic tile, clay paint, and exposed wood ensure a healthy, nontoxic environment.

Preservation of Personal Health

Sourcing materials locally gives you a better sense of their safety. Synthetic paint, carpet, linoleum, plywood, caulk, foam insulation, PVC pipe, and other conventional building products contain hidden toxic components that have been linked to declining personal health. As chemicals have become pervasive in the environment, the incidence of diseases such as cancer has risen. By using local, unprocessed materials you can verify that your home is nontoxic.

A natural home is healthier in two primary ways:

- Synthetic chemicals that pose a health risk are not present
- Clay and straw walls maintain better air quality

Walls experience water from both the outside and the inside. Rain and snow are kept out of the house by the exterior surface. In addition, the difference between inside and outside air pressure can force water into cracks in plaster or siding and around windows.

The ability of air to hold moisture increases with temperature; as the temperature drops, some of the vapor becomes liquid water. Because water vapor moves from high concentrations to low concentrations, it can enter walls, condense, and cause mold and deterioration. The problem we

Making the Case for Natural Timber Frames

encounter in dry climates is that the moisture in a house from bathing, doing laundry, food preparation, and dishwashing fill the air with vapor. Water vapor molecules are smaller than liquid water and thus can get into the smallest crack.

The conventional approach to this problem is to place a vapor barrier, typically a plastic sheet, on the interior surface of the wall to stop vapor before it enters the insulation. In the past, air quality in houses has been fairly good due to poor seals. Wind whistling around doors and windows is an indicator of good air exchange, but also of poor thermal performance. More thoroughly sealed modern dwellings prevent heated air from escaping but lock in toxins that cause health problems.

A vapor barrier is essentially a home-sized plastic bag; the contaminants in the air cannot escape. This presents us with a dilemma: we need fresh air in the house but don't want to lose the heat. The technological fix to the problem is to install an air-to-air heat exchanger. This device uses a fan to force incoming cold air past exiting hot air, adding a good amount of the heat to the incoming fresh air.

The natural approach is to maintain indoor air quality by first eliminating as many sources of contamination as possible. Look for furniture, flooring, paints, and so on without toxic components or volatile organic compounds (VOCs) that off-gas into the interior air.

If critically selected, plants can operate as a natural mechanical system in the house by exchanging carbon dioxide with oxygen and removing other indoor air pollutants. In the resource section of this book, we reference a guide to selecting houseplants that are particularly effective. We encourage you to think of plants as more than decoration.

Clay has the unique ability to pass water vapor but repel liquid water. When rain hits plaster from the exterior, clay molecules swell to block further penetration of the water. Direct rain will eventually overcome the bonding of the clay particles and cause it to erode. For this reason, a good roof overhang and modest wall heights are advisable with exterior clay plasters. In the event of damage, you can simply wet the area and apply more plaster.

On the inside of a wall, clay plaster will take in and release water vapor to regulate indoor humidity levels. And because it will not encounter any barriers, such as plywood or vinyl siding, vapor will slowly pass through a natural wall and transfer to the exterior air.

Finally, clay preserves the wood within the wall. Because it holds a lower equilibrium moisture content than wood, it ensures that water caught in the junction between timber and insulation will be pulled out.

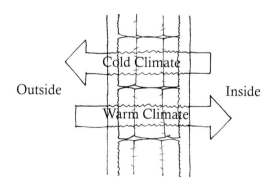

Outside   Cold Climate   Inside

Warm Climate

Natural Wall
Water Vapor Migaration

Making the Case for Natural Timber Frames

Houseplants possess a remarkable
ability to process indoor air pollutants.

Making the Case for Natural Timber Frames

Economic Interactions

By approaching commerce with the idea that we support a set of values each time we open our wallet, we can create an economy that satisfies a broad set of needs.

It is through economic activity that we deplete natural resources and so it is only by reprioritizing our economic activity that

we can save them. The global trade system gives us such a narrow picture of our true impact on the world that our responsibility for material choices appears to begin at the lumberyard.

Yet the problem—even for those who care—is that we lack reliable information.

Because we can't see our impact on the world, we cannot effectively solve the problems we create—we know them only in a very limited sense.

Natural building allows us to participate not just in consumption, but also in creation. By choosing straw over fiberglass, we

Making the Case for Natural Timber Frames

The hands of friends and neighbors assist in raising an English tying joint.

are in a better position to know the sources of materials and the systems they support. Do they support soil conservation and a vibrant local economy or soil erosion and the use of chemical fertilizers? We have the knowledge to be responsible. Whatever material we choose, we do so with a realistic picture of the impacts. When we acknowledge that what we consume in the world is our responsibility, we can then move on to living responsibly.

Straw and timber require limited processing for use in building. The tools to square a timber and cut joinery are simple and relatively inexpensive or can be made by a skilled blacksmith. The craft of timber framing does not inherently support centralization in the way that the production of plywood does because it does not require uniform components; each frame is cut and assembled locally.

Making the Case for Natural Timber Frames

Wood pegs show the connection
between posts and beams.

58   Making the Case for Natural Timber Frames

Local fire-killed wood used for frame, counter, cabinets, and sink.

Making the Case for Natural Timber Frames

A small owner-built timber frame home, with locally sourced wood and earthen plaster, was financed without a mortgage.

Making the Case for Natural Timber Frames

We often overlook the influence of our economic interactions. If we buy from large department stores or big box stores, we "vote" for more than just low price; we endorse one large business over several small ones, money leaving the town instead of being put back into the local economy, and the production of our goods abroad.

By centralizing production and distributing uniform items, the industrial economy reduces diversity in building systems. There are two ways to look at the result: the ability to get the same product anywhere allows us the freedom to use the same building system virtually anywhere or, conversely, if we are all dependent on the same product then everyone is in competition for the same materials.

For example, if you use local Engelmann spruce for your timber frame and wheat straw for the infill, you will not be competing with others for limited supplies of plywood and foam insulation. Like plant communities, we can solve resource problems by becoming better adapted to our place, better able to use what is available to meet our needs.

Depending on the approach taken, the monetary cost of a natural timber frame can range from almost free to much more than a conventional house. A natural structure in the conventional system can be expensive because few builders have experience with natural materials and the work is labor intensive. There are, however, some excellent natural builders creating beautiful, healthy, durable houses. If your budget permits and a qualified builder lives near you, this option may fit your situation.

By using local materials and supplying your own labor, building is within reach for people in a much larger range of income levels. A house that stresses human labor input over purchased industrial materials fits well with a minimal-cash-outlay and maximum-personal-involvement model. Local stone can be acquired in many places for free, but takes some time to install because it lacks uniformity; concrete can be quickly formed and poured by tradespeople but at high monetary cost.

Construction of Your Own Home

Our disconnection from the process of building has opened the door for the less-than-perfect construction practices so common in conventional structures. Because few of us are still involved in building, we have little background with which to judge quality. The focus has turned to appearance. Relying on professional builders has given us less durable houses because there are few economic incentives for the builder in a competitive residential housing industry to spend extra time and money on a high-quality structure that will not be financed or appreciated by the owner. To get quality back, to be able to live in a house that will serve its occupants over many generations, more of us need to get involved in building.

Building a house is within the realm of almost everyone. It is not, however, easy. It requires practice, research, and knowledge-able help. But watching first-time builders quickly become proficient with the motions of moving and smoothing clay plasters gives one the strong sense that we are hardwired for building.

Mistakes are one of our greatest cultural inheritances. Humans have been building natural structures for millennia, learning the how's and why's of different tools and techniques. The inferior approach was made

First-time timber framers participate in a raising.

Making the Case for Natural Timber Frames

By including people of various vocations, ages, and skill levels, a timber frame raising becomes a community event.

obvious by failure or inefficiency, and it set the stage for the better. Workshops, local builders, books, and the Internet hold this accumulated cultural knowledge at our fingertips.

Skills come with experience. As an owner/builder, you may have years of carpentry under your belt or simply have no more than a desire to learn and a thorough collection of home books. Your most important assets are your vision and enthusiasm. Skills can be learned, but even a small house is a big project that requires dedication. Natural building provides a viable option for the owner/builder. The system has less complexity and uses simple, inexpensive tools; and the nontoxic materials are satisfying to work with.

Timber framing and natural building are quite different from conventional construction. A weeklong workshop will likely prove more useful to you than six months on a carpentry crew. Workshops are designed to equip you with a maximum number of skills in a minimum amount of time.

This book lays the philosophical groundwork and equips you with a basic understanding of the materials and techniques that comprise natural timber framing. Yet it is only part of the equation. After reading this book, we recommend the following steps to continue your education before undertaking your first natural home:

1. Search out specific books on design, stone masonry, timber framing, strawbale or clay/straw, and roofing.
2. Attend a timber framing and wall-infill workshop. The time and money spent will be handsomely repaid in the efficiency and confidence you gain.
3. Find owner/builders in your area who will share information. Learn from their mistakes and pay careful attention to what worked for them.
4. Practice. Volunteer to help a friend or neighbor with their project.

The modern house has become a commodity because we have disconnected ourselves from the process of building. We don't see the house as having a story or as being part of our story. Working on your own natural timber frame gives you a much deeper appreciation for your home. The house becomes part of your history. It becomes something sacred.

The hand-hewn frame, soft lime plaster, and thatch roof of this cottage predate the industrialization of building.

Making the Case for Natural Timber Frames

Size of Your Natural Timber Frame Home

One approach to determining how big your natural home should be is to lay out the spaces you feel you need—based on your current standard of living. Another is to set a reasonable limit, 1,200 square feet perhaps, and conclude that it is therefore "green." A third approach is to put house size in the context of available energy.

The energy required to build a house can potentially come from electricity, propane, diesel, gas, or human effort. If you do not use fossil fuels for your house, how do you get the work done? A backhoe can dig holes very quickly by consuming diesel, but how many people would it take to replace it? Twenty or thirty people with shovels? Consider the saws and other power tools. How many people would be needed to replace them? A picture starts to develop showing that we really have quite a large crew on site in the form of fossil fuels.

Building without external power is labor intensive and is the reason that traditional houses are not large. Human energy provides a useful context for sizing a structure. Because the use of fossil fuels is our primary environmental and economic challenge, the size of a sustainable house is one that can be built by the number of people, amount of time, and local resources you have available.

If you were to construct a conventional house—from the foundation to the roof—using only hand tools, it would take an enormous amount of time. Digging a stem-wall trench or mixing concrete by hand would require Herculean effort. Our conventional building system has, to a great extent, developed as a response to the availability of external energy in the form of backhoes, power saws, drills, nail guns, and so on.

Using a system that is consistent with hand-tool technology enables us to build a reasonably sized house by hand. Think about your needs within the context of a fossil-fuel-free building. How can your needs be met in a smaller space through better design? The building system you choose in many ways determines the appropriate tools. For ideas, we can look to the systems of building that developed before machinery, when houses were built in the context described.

Industrial materials, such as Sheetrock and plywood, require flat surfaces for attachment—value is assigned to straightness and flatness by the system. Power tools, like compound miter and table saws, allow for quick replication of the many parts of a conventional house (e.g., studs for a conventionally framed wall). Straw walls lend themselves to human hands because of their sculptural quality. The "right" shape is an aesthetic instead of procedural choice. Plywood asks for flatness; clay leads to articulation. Straightness and replication are not the primary determinants of quality.

Hand tools were used to cut these diagonal brace joints.

Hand Tools Vs. Power Tools

Hand tools are usually slower than their electrical equivalents, but this is relative to the scale of the project. Single cuts here and there may be of comparable speed when you factor in the setup of power tools. An individual person can accomplish large amounts of work in a very short period of time with power tools such as excavators. This can be both good and bad: obviously progress is desirable, but as we have been busy proving over the last century, vast amounts of destruction are not. We have to be very careful when we harness power that is not our own. Soil that formed over thousands of years can be destroyed by a backhoe in an afternoon, resulting in a lifetime restoration project.

Natural timber frames evolved with hands and hand tools. Straw and clay can be shaped without mechanical assistance. To give an associated example, think of your kitchen cabinets. If you live in a typical house, you will see uniform banks of upper and lower boxes. This approach to kitchen storage is a direct result of the table saw, which has made it possible to rip large numbers of uniform pieces of wood. Before power saws, "Hoosier" cabinets or other freestanding furniture was the norm—it was a better fit for craftsmen with hand tools. Trying to build modern cabinets with tools from the 1800s would be a mismatch of systems—certainly possible, but by no means efficient.

To summarize, power tools can increase speed, but at a cost. The type of building system you choose has a direct influence on the extent to which you will need backhoes and table saws. Natural timber framing is a labor-intensive approach to building, which is an advantage if you can provide your own labor, are working within a budget, and wish to eliminate the uses of petroleum.

Making the Case for Natural Timber Frames

The complexity and price of tools has increased with evolving building systems. Labor is typically half of the total house budget. For contractors, time saved by automation is paid back handsomely in reduced costs—offsetting the purchase price and maintenance of power tools. Owner/builders won't have the ongoing jobs to spread the purchase price, so large tool expenditures make less sense.

Hand tools can be found in many antique stores or online auctions. Their quality is usually quite high compared to the modern equivalent. The price is generally very low if the item is not of interest to collectors. New hand tools of high quality are once again becoming available through specialty tool suppliers. Since these items are made to last and perform well, they generally represent a good overall value.

Power tools range widely in price. The less expensive consumer versions of many tools may not even last through one house project and are bound to cause you more headaches than their low price is worth. Think of new cheap tools not as a surprisingly good deal, but as being inexpensive for good reason. Since many power tools are made of plastic and contain delicate electrical parts, their lifespan is fairly limited. You are not going to be passing a cordless drill down to your grandchildren.

Power tools run on either gas or electricity—their manufacture, delivery, and operation add carbon to the atmosphere and further increase our dependence on dwindling resources. Power tools are, as a rule loud, dangerous, and exclusionary—their weight, power, and cost limit their use to specialists.

Chisels and handsaws require only human energy. Since photosynthesis is the engine of the food chain, hand tools are essentially solar powered. The by-product is physical fitness instead of pollution. People without extensive carpentry experience can safely use hand tools.

Renewable human energy powers this hand plane.

Making the Case for Natural Timber Frames

Making the Case for Natural Timber Frames

Beauty of Natural Structures

In our travels, we have been inspired by the richness and character of natural buildings. The subtle undulations of color and shape in clay-plastered walls are soothing when contrasted with the starkness and straightness of drywall and synthetic paint. Timber ages so gracefully. The dings and patina that develop from use over time are now highly sought after in the recycled wood market.

A natural timber frame is a place of both mental and physical refuge. In an age when artificial substitutes are sold for everything from stone to siding, it is very satisfying to build your home from real materials. Wood, stone, clay, and straw are beautiful without trying. They reinforce our connection to the natural world. The subtle textures of timber and clay remind us that we are not just accountants, engineers, or teachers; we are also inhabitants of the earth.

The beauty of natural structures originates in forests and fields instead of factories.

This centrally located adobe wall
provides thermal mass for a
passive solar timber frame home.

Making the Case for Natural Timber Frames

A wood countertop and cabinets with a tile backsplash are nontoxic and attractive.

Making the Case for Natural Timber Frames

The structure itself becomes part of the
decoration in a timber frame home.

Making the Case for Natural Timber Frames

A recycled barn frame behind a claw-foot bathtub.

The pitch of the rafters define a cozy nook for this bed. Natural paints create a personal expression.

Making the Case for Natural Timber Frames

A "truth window" gives a glimpse inside
a strawbale wall.

Getting to Know Our Place

Throughout human history growing food and building shelter have by necessity given us a deep knowledge of place. We discovered which native plants were poisonous, which were edible, and which could be used for medicine. We learned to arrange trees, earth, and stone into dwellings to protect ourselves from rain and snow.

External energy in the form of oil and coal has dramatically changed our relationship to the natural world. It has given us access to commodities from everywhere on earth and by doing so has disconnected us from needing and understanding our place.

Because we rely on grocery stores and lumberyards to supply us with the necessities of life, we now primarily view forests not as the substance of our lives but as scenery.

In exchange for a deep understanding of our place, the industrial economy has given us a shallow understanding of the entire globe. Something valuable has been lost in this trade. We have abundant food, but not good food. We have big houses, but not healthy or welcoming houses. We have fast cars, and little reason to stay home.

Our houses are always seventy-two degrees and fruit is always ripe—we don't experience cycles. The natural world is sometimes dormant yet we live as if we always can and should be able to experience summer. It is quite probable that a cool period is as vital a part of our rhythms as it is to the future blossoms of an apple tree.

To a certain point this is desirable. Few of us in the industrialized world starve in winter. Yet there is no part of our year for preparation, or for slowing down. By ignoring seasonal changes, our current living systems tell us little about our history. We don't see the tremendous impact we have on the ecosystems and climate that make our lives possible. We don't have a time for looking back; we are unaware of our source.

Getting to Know Our Place

The Bioregion

Bioregion is a name for the distinct areas of climate and vegetation that make up your place. Thoroughly evaluating your area is the first step in choosing a building system and a good introduction to your ecosystem.

Bioregionalism is the concept that who we are is inseparable from where we are. Our place shapes buildings, food, and even our perception of the world. But we are still operating with the frontier mentality—using up one place with the hope that we can always "move on." There are, however, fewer places to move on to, and while striking out for distant horizons may work on a personal level, as a culture we have to make all places home.

Bioregional thinking lays out the process in the following manner: If you derive your living from a place, you will come to know that place. Knowing is the first step in caring. If you care about your place, you will take better care of it and it will take care of you.

Many examples exist of communities that have not protected their environment. There is an important difference in the incentives given by acquiring money from the resources of a place and deriving your food, clean water, and building materials

An aspen and pine forest provides wood suitable for timbers, window sash, roof and floor boards, and furniture.

Growth rings show the age and hint at the strength of a tree.

Getting to Know Our Place

directly from a place. Sourcing building materials through a lumberyard takes money. Sourcing materials locally requires healthy ecosystems. The industrial economy encourages the belief that we need money more than trees.

Natural building can be divided into three steps:

1. Get to know your bioregion.
2. Find available materials.
3. Design a house with those materials.

Getting to know your bioregion will give you a sense of its uniqueness, opportunities, and challenges. Go for a hike with a field guide and make a list of the native species. Talk to loggers and private landowners about available timber.

This book specifically addresses the potential uses of wood, clay, stone, straw, and sun. These are the materials for building available in forested bioregions, which cover much of the North American continent.

The maturity of a tree is revealed in the texture of the bark.

Getting to Know Our Place

Wood growth patterns and knots are clearly
expressed in an exposed timber frame joint.

Getting to Know Our Place

Indigenous Materials

WOOD

Wood is the skeleton and the vascular system of a tree. By lifting its light-collecting leaves toward the sky, a tree develops a strong frame to resist wind forces and deliver nutrients to its branches. The strength and lightness of wood is used by us for resisting the snow and wind loads placed on a house.

Because a tree trunk is essentially a bundle of fibers—like a stranded cable—timber has good bending and tensile strength—especially for its weight. Strength and lightness are critical to timber framing because a structure is assembled on the ground and lifted into place. Timber can also be worked with relatively simple hand tools. The handsaw is a cultural achievement, advanced compared to a stone hatchet but simple compared to the complexity of a power saw.

Wood is versatile. An entire house can be built from wood. Finally, wood is exceptionally beautiful as roofing, siding, flooring, timber frames, windows, doors, cabinetry, and furniture.

Timber originates in forests, which are highly dynamic living systems. They provide us with oxygen, food, and shelter, and have profound effects on climate. We cannot live on the earth without forests, but today we tend to regard them only as a source of raw materials for industry, which we essentially mine, or as places to visit on vacation.

A forest regenerates itself. New growth is shown here against old growth.

Fire-killed logs ready to be milled into timber.

Getting to Know Our Place

As a culture we have adopted a win/lose attitude toward forests. The ones near us are often close to our hearts and we speak about protecting them when we can. Yet we still live in houses made of wood that has to come from somewhere. We don't believe that we can have both healthy forests and wood, and the impact of our civilization on living systems appears to support this belief.

Yet we have called upon forests for our needs in the past without compromising their long-term integrity or confining them to national parks. In North America, native people used fire extensively to control plant and animal diseases, increase nut production and game habitat, and to clear brush for a more comfortable living. Many of the primeval forests were essentially a large-scale farming system unrecognizable to European settlers because they had no equivalent.

To make wood use sustainable over the long term, ecosystem health must be our first priority.

So what is a healthy forest? This is a question that scientists, universities, and the logging industry are all trying to answer. Beware of "as healthy as you can expect given that we need all the trees" method of forest management.

Tree plantation with equally spaced rows. Trees are harvested after about a decade and replanted with the same fast-growing species.

Getting to Know Our Place

Here are a few guidelines:

- A healthy forest has a maximum amount of plant, animal, and fungal diversity.
- A healthy forest is structurally diverse and has plants of various ages.
- A healthy forest is selectively thinned—leaving the best-adapted trees to provide a viable gene pool for the future.
- A healthy forest has healthy soil.

Fire suppression and industrial-scale logging have resulted in very unhealthy forests in many parts of the country—disease and insects are taking their toll. As forestry makes an ideological shift from growing trees to a more holistic practice of ecosystem management, there is now opportunity to find usable timber from restoration work. This work involves thinning and controlled burns. Horse loggers are available in some areas to do the heavy work while minimizing forest disturbance.

Selective thinning involves an opportunity for a local wood products revival. Search out local mills and support them. Ask where they get their trees and let them know you care about sustainable forestry.

In a healthy forest, trees are of different ages. Fallen logs decay and provide fertile soil for future generations of trees.

Getting to Know Our Place

A log pinned in place and the tools used to hand hew a timber.

The end of the log is marked with a center line and then the shape of the desired beam is outlined.

Use their services for milling decking and trim and know that the extra you might pay is well spent. If larger local mills aren't available, look for a portable sawmill operator. They may have timber or know of a local source. If your site is treed, a band saw could produce your beams on-site or you could hand hew the timber with a few simple tools. Recycled buildings may provide good wood if you are willing to do some demolition work or happen to have a local wood-products recycler.

Fewer and fewer places have healthy forests. Become acquainted with regional forestry issues and decide when and where logging will be possible and which loggers cut responsibly. It is a possible conclusion that no logging is environmentally sound in your area. If you can't see any tall trees when looking out your window, another building system may be more appropriate for your place. Planting trees for a future timber frame may be an option if you own a piece of land, but obviously this is a long-term approach.

Facing left: Lines are snapped the length of the log to indicate cutting depth.

Facing right above: Notches are cut to the depth of the snapped lines.

Facing right below: Final shaping is done with a broad axe. Cuts are made between notches, leaving a finished timber.

Getting to Know Our Place

Getting to Know Our Place

In many parts of the world, a traveler can get a sense of local geology by looking at houses. Because stone is so heavy, it was traditionally moved only short distances. Mountain towns consequently change character in the same way as the surrounding cliffs. Stone has been used in buildings for millennia—from the pyramids in Egypt to Gothic cathedrals, stone fences, homes, and churches. Structures hundreds and thousands of years old still remain.

Stone is one of the few materials available that can be placed in contact with biologically active soil and remain intact. As homebuilders, we can use foundations of stone to raise timbers twelve or more inches above the fungus and soil organisms that would cause quick decay.

Concrete is widely available, formable to a variety of shapes, and strong when combined with rebar, but these attributes come at a price. Cement kilns use vast amounts of energy and add a correspondingly high amount of carbon to the atmosphere, trucks are needed to transport concrete, and gravel crushers are needed to produce the aggregate. In addition, concrete generally requires some kind of finish over it to make it attractive.

Both cement and stone are produced with large amounts of energy. The distinction is that while stone is formed with earth energy, such as volcanic activity and pressure, cement production uses carbon-emitting fuels, such as coal and oil, that contribute to climate change. Rocks are natural and reusable. Stone is beautiful without further finishing and can be worked with simple tools.

Stone is available in most places and is one of the main reasons that traditional stonework can be found all over the world. Because stone is so heavy, villages are often located near stone sources. There are a couple of advantages to this type of development. First, the builder could use the heaviest material in the house close to its source. Second, rocky areas are typically not the best for farming. By locating dwellings near cliffs or outcroppings, the best lands for food production were protected.

There is a tradeoff between durability and workability in stone. Harder stones, such as granite, are extremely resistant to water absorption and weathering. However, hand shaping of the stones is more labor intensive. Sandstone and limestone are generally softer, and more easily altered with simple steel chisels and hammers, but they may not be as durable.

Dry-stacked, hand-shaped stones create a beautiful, durable wall.

Sandstone is a soft and easily worked stone.

Getting to Know Our Place

Granite is strong and weather resistant.

90

Clay is a generic name for a group of silicate-bearing minerals formed by chemical weathering or hydrothermal activity. Compared with sand and silt, clay particles are much smaller. In the presence of water and pressure, the microscopic flat platelets of clay molecules chemically bond.

Clay is sticky. Applied to the interior and exterior of strawbale or clay/straw walls, clay plaster allows vapor transmission but prohibits the intrusion of liquid water, protecting the insulating layer beneath. If hit by rain, clay particles quickly swell, sealing the wall and inhibiting further water penetration.

Because it expands when wet, pure clay applied to the wall surface cracks as it dries. By adding fiber for tensile strength and sand to reduce shrinkage, the resulting clay plaster is a strong composite material. Clay can be fired and glazed to make bricks and waterproof roof tiles. Mixed with straw, woodchips, or other cellulose fiber, it provides an insulating wall. Clay plaster adds thermal mass and strength and provides excellent fire resistance.

Like wood, clay has a long history as a building material. And also like wood, clay is versatile. It has been used for walls, roofs, floors, and plaster; entire structures are sometimes made of clay in areas without stone or wood.

Mineral subsoil is composed of sand, silt, or clay—or a mix of the three. Topsoil contains decaying organic matter, microorganisms, and plant roots. The dark upper layer of soil has too much organic matter for plaster. Save it for the garden. Six to eight inches below—in the subsoil—is where to begin your search. Look for places that leave a shiny surface when you dig with a shovel. Soil that has a "sticky" feeling may contain adequate quantities of clay for building.

Gravel pits are a likely source of clay. Topsoil and subsoil are stripped away to expose gravel used in concrete and road construction. Called "overburden" by miners, clay is generally considered a waste product and clay-bearing soil may be available for a few dollars a cubic yard plus the cost of trucking. Road cuts and other residential construction sites are potential sources.

To test a sample for clay content, take a handful of damp clay or add water to dry soil to get a bread dough consistency. Roll the dampened soil between your palms into a pencil shape. If the sample is elastic enough to bend completely around your finger without breaking, it has sufficient clay content for building use.

The drop test is another good way to determine clay content. Add water to a soil sample and roll it into a ball. It should be shiny, sticky, and smooth. From shoulder height, drop the ball on a hard surface. If the sample fractures or explodes it has low clay content; if fine cracks appear on the surface but the mass is still intact, it will make a good building material.

A third approach is the jar test. Take a mason jar filled one-third with water, add soil until it is two-thirds full, and shake vigorously. The sample will settle out in layers with course rocks and sand dropping to the bottom almost immediately. The silt layer takes fifteen minutes to an hour to form and clay will remain in suspension for several hours. Organic matter will float. An ideal sample is one that remains cloudy for several hours and has a large upper, or clay, layer.

Follow other tests with an application of clay slip (water-and-clay mix) to a strawbale. Good clay will dry hard without dusting and will not easily rub off.

Clay in its pure form cracks and shrinks as it dries.

Getting to Know Our Place

Baled straw gives a natural wall insulation and strength.

STRAW

Straw is the dry stalk of a cereal plant, such as wheat, barley, or rice, left after the grain or seed has been removed. Straw matures in one short growing season—about three or four months. It is hollow and lightweight, providing good insulation. And similar to wood, straw fibers run in a single direction, adding tensile strength to walls and plasters. Composed mostly of cellulose, straw is much more resistant to decay than hay, which includes seeds, green leaves, and other nitrogen-rich components.

Straw is unique in our list of materials because it is an agricultural product. It is often grown on land treated with chemical fertilizers and herbicides. Like tree plantations, wheat fields have almost no biodiversity or natural stability. Look for straw that is organically grown on small mixed-crop farms. These soils are fertilized with manure and compost and often have a mix of plant and animal species, resulting in a much more resilient landscape.

As with logging practices, we need to be careful of overharvesting. Straw is not a waste product as is sometimes claimed because the nutrients in the stalk are needed by the soil for food. Fungi and other soil organisms can break down the stalk and restore to the soil some of the minerals that were used to produce the grain. By removing the straw from the field, we are essentially clear-cutting the vegetation. Other ways of managing fertility may be needed, such as adding manure or compost or rotating crops. Cutting native grass straw after the plant has gone to seed and dried may be an option.

When appropriately utilized, straw provides:

- a self-supporting wall
- excellent insulation
- slow vapor migration through the wall without damage
- wind and earthquake resistance
- a base for plaster

Mature barley before harvest.

A tractor with a mechanical baler that
gathers and ties the straw into rectangular form.

Getting to Know Our Place

A farmer with draft animals moving bales to the building site.

SUN

The sun is the starting point of all life. Solar radiation not only provides heat and light to the earth, but also drives photosynthesis. With appropriate orientation and design, a house relies less on artificial lights and fossil-fuel-burning heaters and more on the free energy of the sun.

When designing a passive solar house, consider the need to:

- allow solar energy to enter the house
- store the additional heat in thermal mass
- retain heat in the house

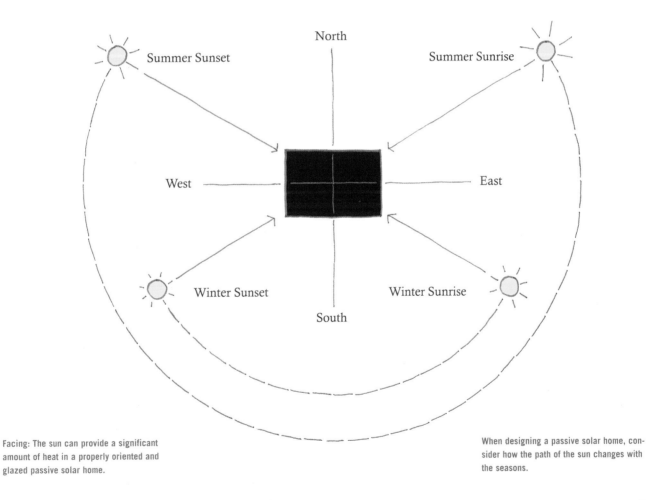

Facing: The sun can provide a significant amount of heat in a properly oriented and glazed passive solar home.

When designing a passive solar home, consider how the path of the sun changes with the seasons.

Allow Solar Energy to Enter the Building

In the northern hemisphere, the sun enters east-facing glass in the morning, south-facing at midday, and west-facing in the evening. North-facing windows receive little direct energy, but do provide light. Horizontal overhangs sized to admit the low winter sun, but exclude the higher summer sun can control excessive heat gain from the south. About half of your window area should be on the south to take advantage of solar gain.

Store the Additional Heat

Dense materials, such as stone and clay plaster, absorb and release heat slowly, preventing big temperature swings in a house. Placed on a floor or wall inside the building, this thermal mass will act as a reservoir—filling up with the heat energy when the sun is present and slowly giving it back to the space when the sun is at rest. The incoming solar energy has to heat something; without thermal mass it will heat the air. By locating stone or clay walls and floors so the rays of the low winter sun hit them, the excess heat will be stored for release at night without overheating the interior air.

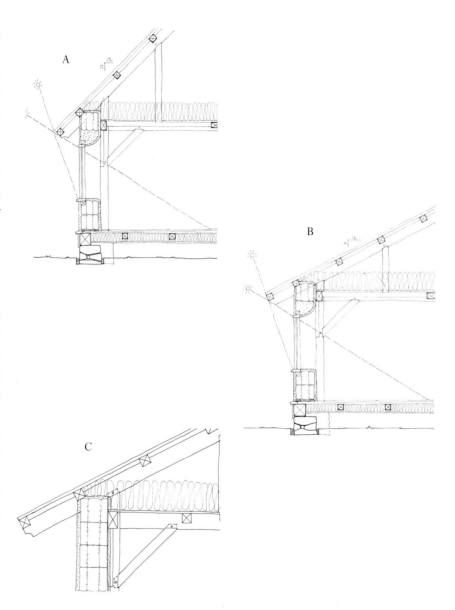

(A) The high pitch of this roof brings the eave closer to the building. The overhang is sized to admit the sun's rays in winter and prevent overheating in summer. (B) A lower roof pitch extends the roof farther from the building and affords greater protection from weather. The roof is also optimized for passive solar benefit. (C) Detail showing how timber frame and strawbale walls intersect and provide for ceiling insulation that carries the thermal envelope entirely around the building.

Getting to Know Our Place

A framed south-facing wall allows for passive solar gain, and strawbale walls retain the heat within the building.

Insulation keeps the added heat from conducting through the wall to the exterior. Careful detailing of the joints between materials prevents heated interior air from flowing directly out of the house. Insulate the windows, floors, walls, and ceiling of the inhabited space.

Strawbale or light clay/straw provide good wall insulation with the use of local materials. The natural timber frame should also be insulated from below in the cavities formed by the floor joists. Wool is a good choice for insulation. Because heat rises, adding a generous amount of insulation to the roof area makes economic sense. The structure we describe in the last chapter has a flat, timbered platform to provide deep roof insulation.

Glass is the nexus of passive solar heating. Heat received through glazing can be lost with equal rapidity at night because glass is a poor insulator. Double glazing and insulating shutters or thermal curtains can prevent heat escape at night when no energy is being gained through windows. Insulated glass will significantly reduce interior condensation during cold months.

Glazing set into wall and protected from rain by projected head detail.

Sheep are a source of renewable insulation.

Putting It All Together

Using a modestly sized timber frame with a dry stone foundation and straw walls as a model, this chapter illustrates how locally available materials can be organized into a house. The drawings presented are not intended as the definitive approach to natural timber framing, but as a place to begin designing a house suitable for your bioregion. We have developed a structure that can be built without fossil fuels, is adaptable to a variety of needs and preferences, is small enough to be a reasonable project for a couple, and relies on locally available and natural materials. You can alter its size, layout, and materials to fit your personal needs and locally available materials.

Wood post-and-beam house with earthen-plastered strawbale walls.

A Plan

In a general sense, developing a plan is the work of figuring out how a house will be used and how the house will be built. What materials will you choose? Who will do the work? How will it be paid for? The previous chapters have outlined the reasons we believe it is important to think more critically about these questions and to evaluate our needs, desires, and assumptions in a broader environmental and economic context.

More specific to the house construction itself is the process of working out the details. Developing a set of construction drawings provides you with a roadmap for each phase of the work, establishes dimensions, and relates materials to one another. Because rafters carry snow loads to the foundation and the foundation supports the posts that hold up the roof, the parts of the house cannot be designed in isolation. All parts of the building are related. A decision made at the bottom affects everything above. "Figuring it out as you go along" makes predicting future details difficult and often results in the builders having to rework previously installed materials. Paper is the best place to make mistakes. Carefully considered details—proven to be workable with a pencil—will make construction much more efficient.

Several books cover the specifics of timber framing, strawbale and clay/straw wall systems, and dry stonework (see the resources section for suggested titles). In this chapter, we discuss the interactions of these systems. We present dry (un-mortared) stonework as a solution to the host of problems created by conventional foundation systems. With drawings, we illustrate how a traditional timber frame floor system can be adapted to resist the forces of wind and earthquakes. To achieve greater energy efficiency in natural building, we discuss issues surrounding the placement of straw walls relative to the timber frame and the importance of a deep insulation cavity in the roof structure. We survey roofing materials that have proven durable through centuries of use, are stunning to look at, and can be produced locally. Finally, we present four sample floor plans to give you a sense of the natural timber frame as a whole.

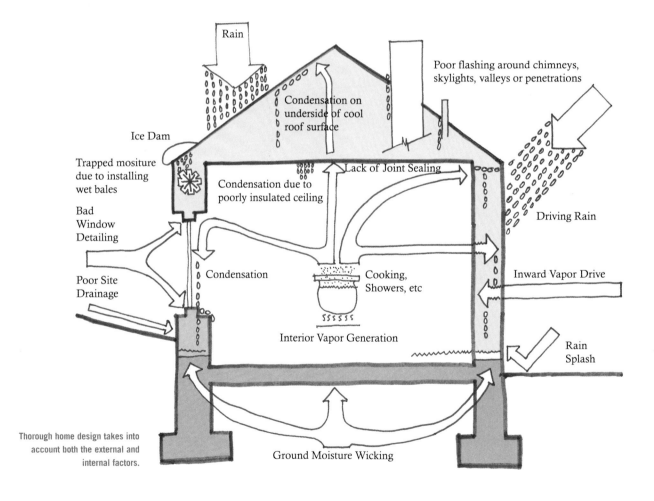

Rain

Poor flashing around chimneys, skylights, valleys or penetrations

Condensation on underside of cool roof surface

Ice Dam

Trapped mositure due to installing wet bales

Lack of Joint Sealing

Condensation due to poorly insulated ceiling

Driving Rain

Bad Window Detailing

Condensation

Cooking, Showers, etc

Inward Vapor Drive

Poor Site Drainage

Interior Vapor Generation

Rain Splash

Thorough home design takes into account both the external and internal factors.

Ground Moisture Wicking

Putting It All Together

Purpose of Foundations

Natural materials like wood and straw will provide strength and insulation almost indefinitely if they are kept dry. However, as soon as the wall or frame comes into contact with soil, fungus and bacteria begin their work of turning the house into food for a new generation of trees. A long-lasting house is one that stays dry—not as simple as it sounds when water moves as vapor.

Keeping your house protected from moisture begins at its connection to the ground. A well-designed foundation system eliminates water problems by:

- extending the foundation to a height above the ground that keeps rain splatter and snow from directly coming into contact with the wall

- providing a capillary break between the foundation and bottom of wall
- preventing condensation from deteriorating the sills and floor system

A comparison of a conventional and a dry stone foundation illustrates the importance of a whole-system approach to building.

A mortared stone foundation supports this timber frame, with an earth and lime plaster infill and a thatch roof.

Concrete footings are located below the depth of frost to ensure that the powerful expansive force of frozen water does not cause structural problems by "heaving" or lifting the house. In northern climates, this depth averages 32 to 48 inches. A typical concrete foundation consists of a separately poured wide footing to distribute the weight of the house into the soil and a tall stem wall to extend the foundation out of the ground. Because concrete is relatively weak in tension, it is poured wet over a matrix of steel rebar. To seal out water, a petrochemical membrane is typically applied to the exterior of the stem wall, followed by gravel or a dimpled plastic drainage layer covered with a geo-textile fabric to prevent soil from clogging the water passages.

Heavy equipment is used for the digging. A backhoe needs at least 20 feet to each side of the building's footprint to maneuver. The soil from the excavation is moved aside and mixed with topsoil when the foundation is backfilled. The ready-mix truck needs that much space as well or the wet concrete will have to be transported by wheelbarrow. A pump truck could also be called in to deliver the wet concrete from the ready-mix truck to the foundation forms, but at a steep additional cost.

Conventional foundations require heavy equipment to dig out soil to the depth of the frost line.

106

Transit mix concrete truck in the background and a tradesman working a slab.

Modular steel forms are used by concrete trades people. Plywood and framing lumber are typically used by the owner/builder. Because of the high cost of steel forms, they are only practical if you intend to build multiple houses. Wood formwork, however, results in a large quantity of waste; concrete-coated plywood will quickly dull tool blades and so is generally impractical to use elsewhere in the building.

This is the conventional foundation system. Depending on your location, it may be the only commercially available option. There are, however, several problems.

For every ton of cement produced, an equal weight of carbon dioxide is released into the atmosphere. Considering the increase in storms and disease, reduction in biodiversity, loss of stable farmland, and other negative impacts of climate change recorded and predicted by scientists to worsen, the pollution associated with cement is the most compelling reason for us to use other foundation systems.

After the house is built, healthy topsoil is necessary for vigorous lawns, trees, and gardens. The disturbance, mixing, and compaction of soil by heavy equipment, however, can set natural soil formation back centuries or even millennia.

Because concrete wicks moisture through capillary action, treated wood or a rot-resistant species is needed if it is to come in direct contact with the foundation. Treated wood contains toxic chemicals that have personal health and environmental consequences. Redwood and cedar perform well as sill plates, but are being cut at an unsustainable rate.

It is impractical to save money by digging a conventional foundation by hand unless you have an extraordinary amount of time and endurance or many, many strong friends. Concrete, labor, trucking, excavating, and eventual site restoration add considerably to the price of a finished house.

If we determine that concrete foundation systems are undesirable or the products not available, how can we build?

The zone of ground disruption of a standard foundation compared to that of the dry-stacked stone system.

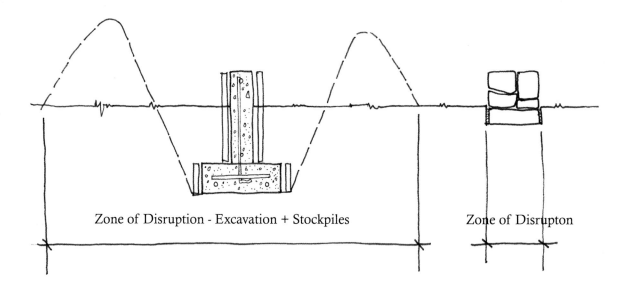

Zone of Disruption - Excavation + Stockpiles

Zone of Disrupton

DRY-STACKED STONE FOUNDATION SYSTEM

Traditionally, timber frames sat on a foundation of stone—ranging from minimally shaped dry stone (masonry without mortar) to lime or clay-mortared ashlar (squared and smoothed blocks). Masons used whatever stone was locally available, but types that fractured into flat planes for more solid stacking and worked easily with hand tools were preferred.

The natural timber frame uses a low-cost foundation system that draws on local materials, has low embodied energy, requires minimal site disturbance, and can be constructed with simple hand tools. It is constructed of dry stone with timber sills and floor joists. Two-inch decking boards lock the entire floor together. The stonework distributes the weight of the building and holds it off the ground; the wood floor system keeps the structure from pulling apart, distributes point loads to the foundation, and acts as a beam to allow a slight rise and fall during freeze/thaw cycles without damaging the structure.

We have adapted the traditional dry stone foundation for earthquakes and high wind, which could potentially shift the house off the foundation. To compensate for these forces, the large stones under the timber

Small "chinking" stones fill the spaces between the larger stones and create a strong and beautiful dry-stacked wall.

frame posts also serve as ballast, holding the structure in place. Based on local wind exposure and seismic zones, an engineer can calculate the weight of stone required behind the timber sills.

Structures with large, complex floor plans would likely suffer on a dry stone foundation because timbers long enough and large enough to evenly support the weight of such a house would be hard to find. As a beam gets longer, the force acting on it increases by its cube—meaning that doubling the length of a beam increases the force on it by a factor of eight. If you need more space, design a house that combines two smaller structures to limit the force on the sills and take advantage of smaller diameter trees.

Because dry stonework does not use mortar, air circulation around the sills helps protect the wood from decay. The small spaces between stones in traditional foundations help break the capillary action that wicks moisture in concrete.

For the dry stone foundation, topsoil is removed with a shovel and placed in the garden or saved for landscaping. Stones are then laid directly on the subsoil and brought up 12 inches or more above the ground. Site disturbance is very minimal, local stone can be used, embodied energy is low, no formwork is required, hand tools can accomplish all parts of the job, and the cost is minimal.

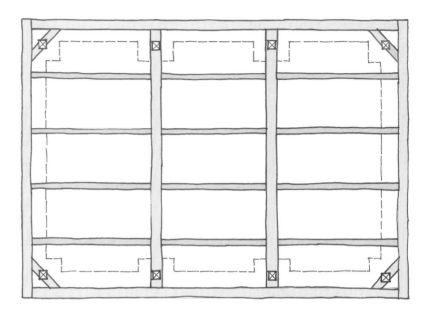

Timber frame sill plates shown above the stone foundation.

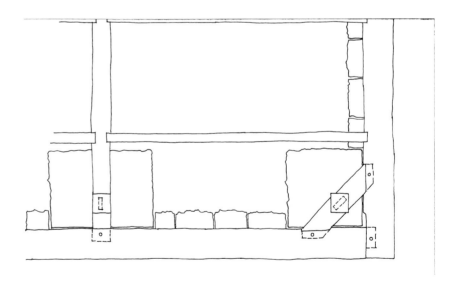

Plan detail showing the position of posts, sill plates, and floor joists above the dry stone foundation. Larger stones at the post locations carry the vertical loads and resist lateral movement by wind and earthquake.

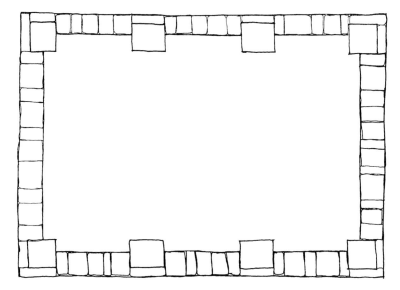

Plan layout of dry stone foundation with larger stones at post locations.

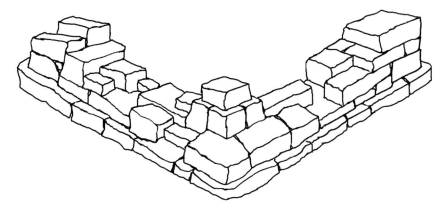

Isometric cutaway of dry-stacked foundation.

Putting It All Together

Hand-cut brace mortices on fir posts.

112

Timber Frame Plus Natural Walls

A timber frame uses wooden joinery and hardwood pegs to connect the various parts of a house: beams, posts, rafters, girts, joists, braces, and sills. There are no nails or bolts used in the frame, and it can be cut with a chisel, mallet, framing square, and handsaw.

Timber frames were historically in-filled between posts with wattle and daub, a heavy plaster applied over woven willow. This wall provided a buffer from the elements, but due to the high sand and clay content provided little in the way of insulation. Also, the joint between timber posts and plaster allowed hot air to escape because the expansion and contraction of wood creates a seasonal gap.

The natural timber frame's insulation is located outside of the wood structure to provide a continuous thermal envelope and allow the wood to remain protected from weather and visible on the interior. Strawbale and clay/straw walls provide much better insulation than wattle and daub because of their high proportion of straw. We have adapted traditional sill design to allow the posts to set in from the edge of the sills and to provide a shelf for the straw wall to rest on.

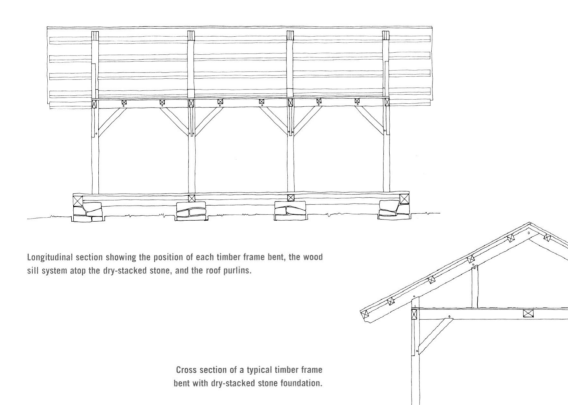

Longitudinal section showing the position of each timber frame bent, the wood sill system atop the dry-stacked stone, and the roof purlins.

Cross section of a typical timber frame bent with dry-stacked stone foundation.

Three knee braces intersect with the post. The joinery is aligned to one side of the post to make hand cutting of the housing easier.

Volunteers spend two hours of their Saturday morning to assist in the assembly of this small Douglas Fir frame.

A fully assembled timber frame with completed roof provides weather protection for the natural wall.

A "commander," or large wooden mallet, is used to seat the joinery.

Putting It All Together

STRAWBALE

While the use of grass-family plant fiber for building has a long history, strawbale construction is relatively new. The availability of mechanical baling machines combined with a lack of wood in late-nineteenth-century Nebraska led to the construction of baled straw homes. Stacked like bricks and protected inside and out with plaster, the bales provided a well-insulated, low-cost dwelling.

To build a wall, the bales are assembled on the top of the sill plates in a running bond, keeping joints above the center of the

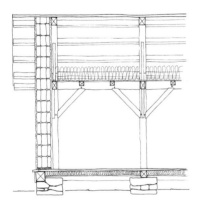

Eave side wall detail shows how strawbales can form a gable wall.

Posts and beams support the roof and strawbales are attached securely to the posts.

Putting It All Together

Volunteers with little or no building experience working together to assemble strawbale walls.

bale below. Light wood framing is used at door and window locations and nailed to the timber frame for stability. The strawbales are notched around the wood framing. Two small-diameter poles, such as willow or bamboo, are tied vertically at each bale to align the wall. These are secured to the sill plate below and timbers above. The wall is then plastered to protect it from the elements and to block rodents.

Strawbales have excellent thermal properties due to their low density. Without clay or sand in the wall, heat loss due to conduction is minimal. In addition, the modular bale can be quickly installed. Clay plaster keys directly to bales without the need for metal netting or other reinforcement.

Minimal framing is required to hold windows in place. Shelter for the top of the window will protect it from weather.

Putting It All Together

A natural timber frame and strawbale wall await earthen plaster.

Clay/straw walls ready for earthen plaster.

Putting It All Together

CLAY/STRAW

Clay/straw has its roots in Germany where it has been used for centuries as a timber frame infill material. Robert LaPorte of Santa Fe, New Mexico, has pioneered its use in the United States.

To construct the clay/straw wall, loose straw is mixed with slip—a mixture of clay and water that is about the consistency of whole milk—until the fibers are well coated. The mix is then placed into a light formwork and tamped into place with feet to provide the pressure necessary to bond the clay particles.

The clay/straw wall uses straw in its loose form, so any size or tightness of bale will work. Woodchips and other cellulose fibers can be used as well. By randomly tangling the fibers, the clay/straw wall interrupts the convection that can occur through the hollow stem of straw, resulting in a better than expected R-value. Because the mix is placed wet, it can be molded around wood framing and utilities. The monolithic nature gives the clay/straw wall inherent strength.

Because the straw is installed wet, it must be given sufficient warm, dry weather to completely dry. October is not a good time to install a clay/straw wall because the cold air will dramatically slow evaporation and encourage mold. Drying will take two or more months depending on ambient temperature and humidity.

After drying, the clay/straw wall provides an ideal base for plaster because of its clay content, which bonds to the clay in the plaster, and its irregularity or "tooth." Because the wall is relatively flat, it can be covered with less than an inch of plaster.

Wood frame is exposed between recently installed clay/straw walls.

Putting It All Together

Clay plaster is an excellent covering for a straw wall. It is a mix of sand, straw, and clay. Sand provides hardness and prevents cracking. Straw adds some flexibility and tensile strength. Clay sticks it all together and provides some resistance to moisture.

Plaster protects the wall from rain, air infiltration, fire, and critters. Clay plaster is vapor permeable and so allows the wall to breathe, or have the potential to dry. A clay plaster wall can be easily repaired if it gets hit by hail or otherwise erodes.

To prepare clay for plaster, remove organic materials, large rocks, and clods by passing the soil through a 1/4-inch screen. Place water in a mixing container and slowly add the sifted clay until several "islands" appear on the surface. Let it sit for ten minutes, in which time the clay will become hydrated, taking on the appearance of thick chocolate milk. Mix with a hoe to incorporate any surface water. This is clay slip. It can be applied directly to a strawbale wall as an adhesive coat or combined with sand and chopped straw to make plaster.

Plaster is built up in layers. The base coat is the thickest. It typically has a high proportion of straw for flexibility and clay for stickiness. The next coat is the scratch

Clay is screened to remove rocks and organic matter prior to making plaster.

coat or brown coat. This layer smoothes out the base coat to the desired final wall shape and contains more sand to reduce potential cracking and provide a stable base for the final layer. It is "scratched" with a comb-like tool to create a mechanical key for the finish coat. The finish coat is of finer sand and clay and shorter straw fibers. Applied in a thin layer, this final coat fills in the scratches in the brown coat. Clay paint applied to this final layer provides a beautiful and easily repairable finish.

Clay plaster is nontoxic, weather resistant, and easily repairable. The application of plaster consumes no fossil fuels, and it can be applied by hand with simple, inexpensive tools.

Right: Plaster can be mixed in a wheelbarrow and easily moved around the job site.

Facing: Earthen plaster being applied to a strawbale wall by the owner and friends.

Putting It All Together

Putting It All Together

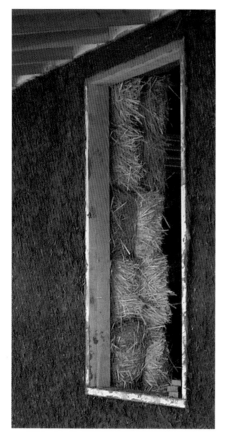

Base coat of plaster applied to the exterior strawbale surface.

The final coat can be burnished to a smooth and weather-resistant surface with a steel trowel.

126

Earthen-plaster wall with wood window.

Dark natural-pigment clay paint complements the
wood frame.

Putting It All Together

Roofs

The cover over your natural timber frame is critical to its longevity. Roofs experience more direct UV radiation, snow, and rain than any other part of the house. A roof in disrepair will quickly lead to structural problems as a result of moisture. A natural timber frame will last for centuries under a good roof.

As with the materials for the rest of the natural timber frame, we encourage you to think locally about roofing materials.

Depending on your bioregion, some natural roof options are:

- wood shake
- stone
- clay tile
- thatch

Wood Shake

Shakes are split rather than sawn out of a block of wood. Almost all wood species that split easily have at one time or another been used as roofing, but the most common are pine, white oak, and cedar. Pine trunks grow with whorls or clumps of branches with clear sections of wood in between. Cutting out the knots leaves clear wood that can be split into shingles with a mallet and an L-shaped tool called a froe. Air circulation under shakes is very important for their longevity. Shakes are laid in an overlapping pattern like other shingles.

Wood shakes can be split from straight-grained wood with simple tools.

Putting It All Together

STONE

Stone, and especially slate, has a long history of use as roofing. Slates are hand split from quarried blocks and punched with nail holes. They are applied like shakes and secured with wooden pegs or copper nails. Because good slate absorbs very little water, roofs can last hundreds of years.

Although slate is the most common, other types of stone have been used for roofing. Local stone that absorbs little water, fractures into thin pieces, and is relatively strong may provide a durable roof.

Stone roofing weathers very slowly and develops a beautiful patina with age.

Clay roof tiles come in a variety of shapes and colors.

Putting It All Together

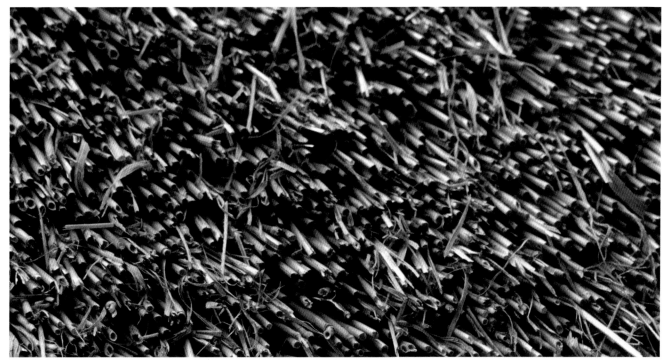

Detail of exposed thatch ends.

CLAY TILE

Clay tiles are a special case because they are fired in a kiln to become waterproof. The energy for firing typically comes from fossil fuels although the potential exists for regional clay roof tile production with renewable wood energy. There is a long history of clay tile use all over the world. Tiles can provide long-lasting, durable, beautiful roofs.

THATCH

Many cultures have a tradition of using straw or water reed to cover their homes. The fiber is tied in bundles and secured to roof purlins. Thatch roofs are not common in dry climates, likely due to fire danger and lack of quality water reeds. An advantage of thatch is that it both sheds water and provides insulation. Thatch must have air circulation under it to prevent deterioration. A well-thatched roof has a lifespan in the forty- to one-hundred-year range. The work is labor intensive, but the finished product is stunning and can be replaced with local materials.

Thatch roofs lend themselves to rounded shapes.

132 Putting It All Together

Floor Plans

We have taken you through the problems of conventional building, the solutions offered by natural materials, and the importance of thinking and living locally. We have attempted to understand the complexity of the construction industry by reducing it to its parts. Our thoughts have moved from the world to the community, to the personal—a transition from large to small.

The physical act of building directs us in the opposite direction. The details work towards the whole. Small rocks laid one by one make up a foundation. Timbers are connected to complete a frame, bales are stacked, and plaster applied in layers. A house develops more clarity with each swing of the mallet and each pass of the chisel.

Building is the work of putting together the pieces of a house in a way that fits your needs, preferences, lifestyle, skills, money, time, and location.

View from the kitchen looking toward the living room, with the dining room at the left. Natural colors give a warm ambiance to the space.

To assist you in this process, we have provided four natural timber frame floor plans. They are intended to demonstrate the variety possible in a 600-square-foot living space and encourage you to think in terms of efficiency. Our sample timber frame is 20 x 30 feet with four bents. This layout creates three equal 10 x 20 bays or six 10 x 10 rooms that can be used as presented or adapted to your specific needs.

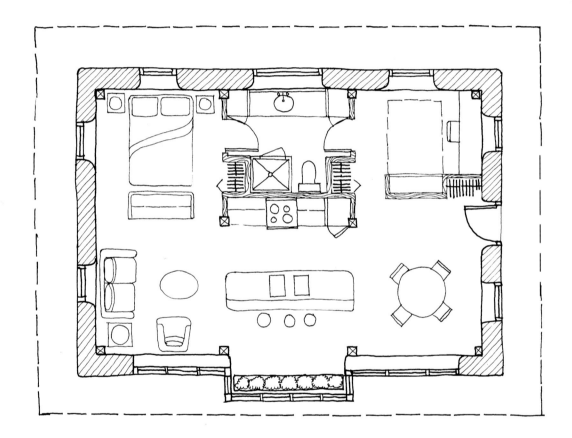

Floor Plan Scheme A

A central bath, which backs the kitchen for ease of plumbing connections, is accessible from both the sleeping area and study. The study in the upper right acts as a second sleeping area when the Murphy bed is lowered. A solar bump-out provides a place for growing edible plants within reach of the cook. Living and dining areas are on the south side of the building, taking advantage of the passive solar glazing.

A rectangular dining and living space, with woodstove and adobe wall to provide thermal mass for the passive south-facing window.

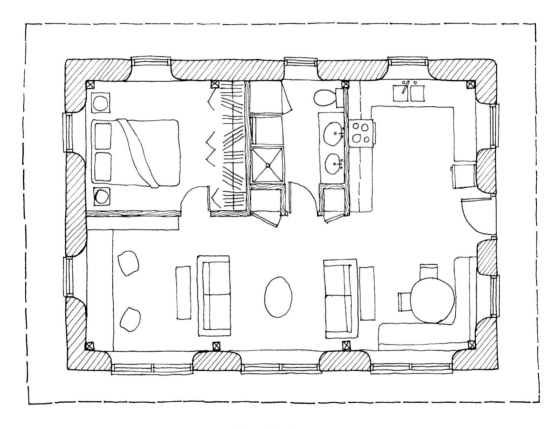

Floor Plan Scheme B

Scheme B differs from Scheme A in several ways. The sleeping space is defined more privately with a partition, and there is a larger wardrobe. The bathroom is accessible centrally and provides storage space. The kitchen is larger and is located conveniently to the dining space situated in the southeast corner to take advantage of morning and midday light. The living area is centered in the space, and a study occupies the west space.

Detail of natural paints and timber frame joinery, with gently curved knee brace and houseplant to enhance indoor air quality.

Putting It All Together

A Japanese room demonstrates the level of sophistication and beauty possible with natural materials.

Putting It All Together

The bar allows the cook to serve meals directly from the kitchen. Windows on two sides of the kitchen provide ample natural light.

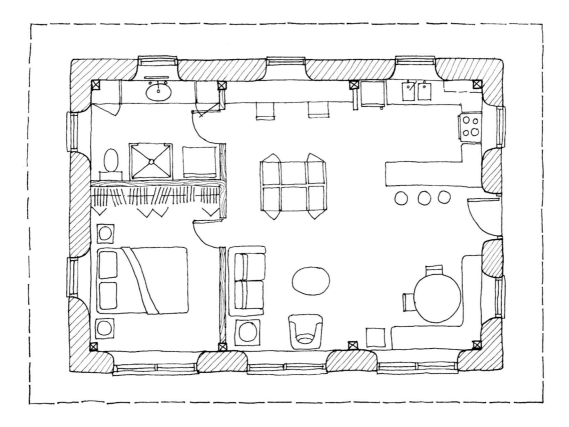

Floor Plan Scheme C

Sleeping and bathing spaces are contained within the western bay. This arrangement allows one great room with study on the north, kitchen to the northeast, entry to the east, and dining room to the southeast. The living room is central and takes advantage of the southern sun.

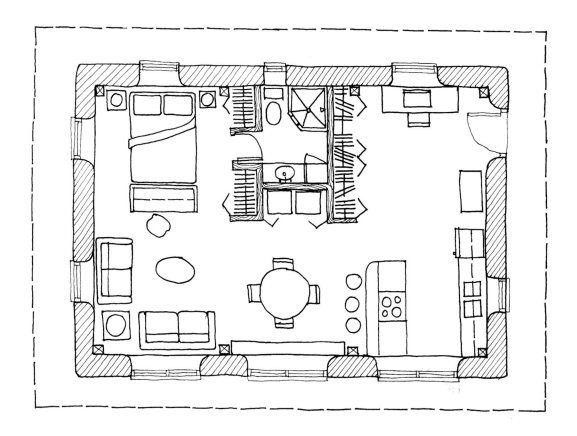

Floor Plan Scheme D

The sleeping area is separated from the living room with a moveable piece of furniture. A small bath is backed up to a laundry area. The study is on the north with a storage wall and the entry. The living room, dining space, and kitchen all share south-facing windows that receive passive solar energy.

Putting It All Together

A hammer-beam truss cut from reclaimed Douglas fir adds visual interest and allows for a larger span between posts. The black marks show where metal fasteners connected these timbers in the original structure.

Putting It All Together

Resources

Timber Frame

Sobon, Jack A. *Build a Classic Timber-Framed House: Planning & Design / Traditional Materials / Affordable Methods.* North Adams, MA: Storey Publishing, 1994.

Sobon, Jack A. *Historic American Timber Joinery: A Graphic Guide.* Becket, MA: Timber Framers Guild, 2001.

Sobon, Jack A., and Roger Schroeder. *Timber Frame Construction: All about Post and Beam Building.* North Adams, MA: Storey Publishing, 1984.

Strawbale

Steen, Bill, Athena Swentzell Steen, and Wayne J. Bingham. *Small Strawbale: Natural Homes, Projects & Designs.* Salt Lake City, UT: Gibbs Smith, Publisher, 2005.

The Last Straw Journal
PO Box 22706
Lincoln, NE 68542
www.thelaststraw.org

Clay/Straw

Baker-Laporte, Paula, and Robert Laporte. *EcoNest: Creating Sustainable Sanctuaries of Clay, Straw, and Timber.* Salt Lake City, UT: Gibbs Smith, Publisher, 2005.

Plaster

Guelberth, Cedar Rose, Dan Chiras, and Deanne Bednar. *The Natural Plaster Book: Earth, Lime, and Gypsum Plasters for Natural Homes.* Gabriola Island, BC, Canada: New Society Publishers, 2002.

Stone

Dry Stone Conservancy
1065 Dove Run Rd., Ste. 6
Lexington, KY 40502
www.drystone.org

Bioregion

Sale, Kirkpatrick. *Dwellers in the Land: The Bioregional Vision.* Athens, GA: University of Georgia Press, 2000.

Air Quality

Wolverton, B. C. *How to Grow Fresh Air: 50 Houseplants That Purify Your Home or Office.* NY: Penguin, 1997.